Interdimensional Portals

A Meditative Adult Coloring Book

Tray Ford

Introduction

Interdimensional Portals is meant to inspire relaxation and mediation. The very act of coloring these flowing forms is hypnotic.

This book strives to help build your patience in a very fulfilling way. So step into a new dimension and flow right into infinity.

ISBN-13: 978-1543068269

Dedicated to
those who have cosmic
dreams.

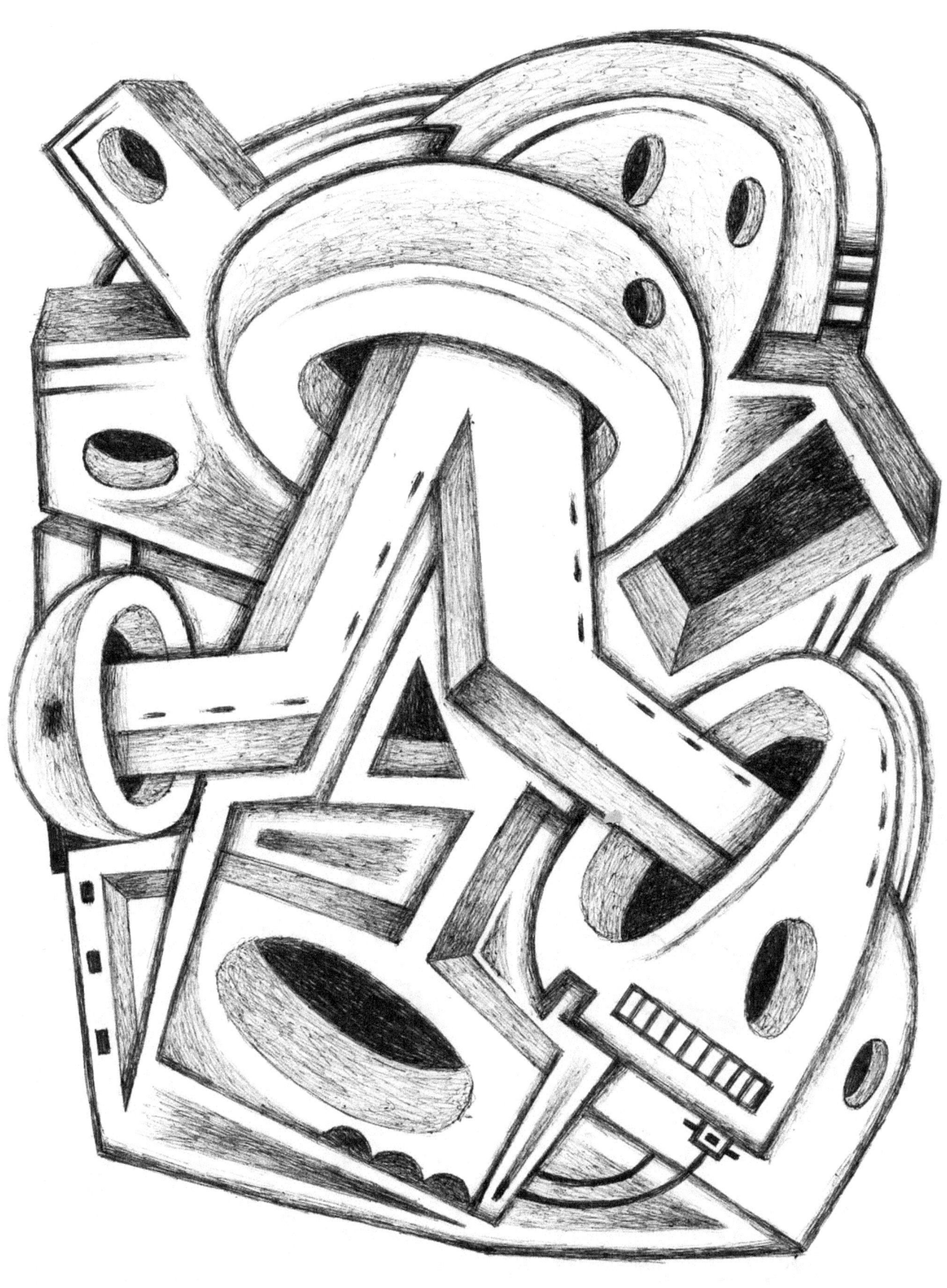

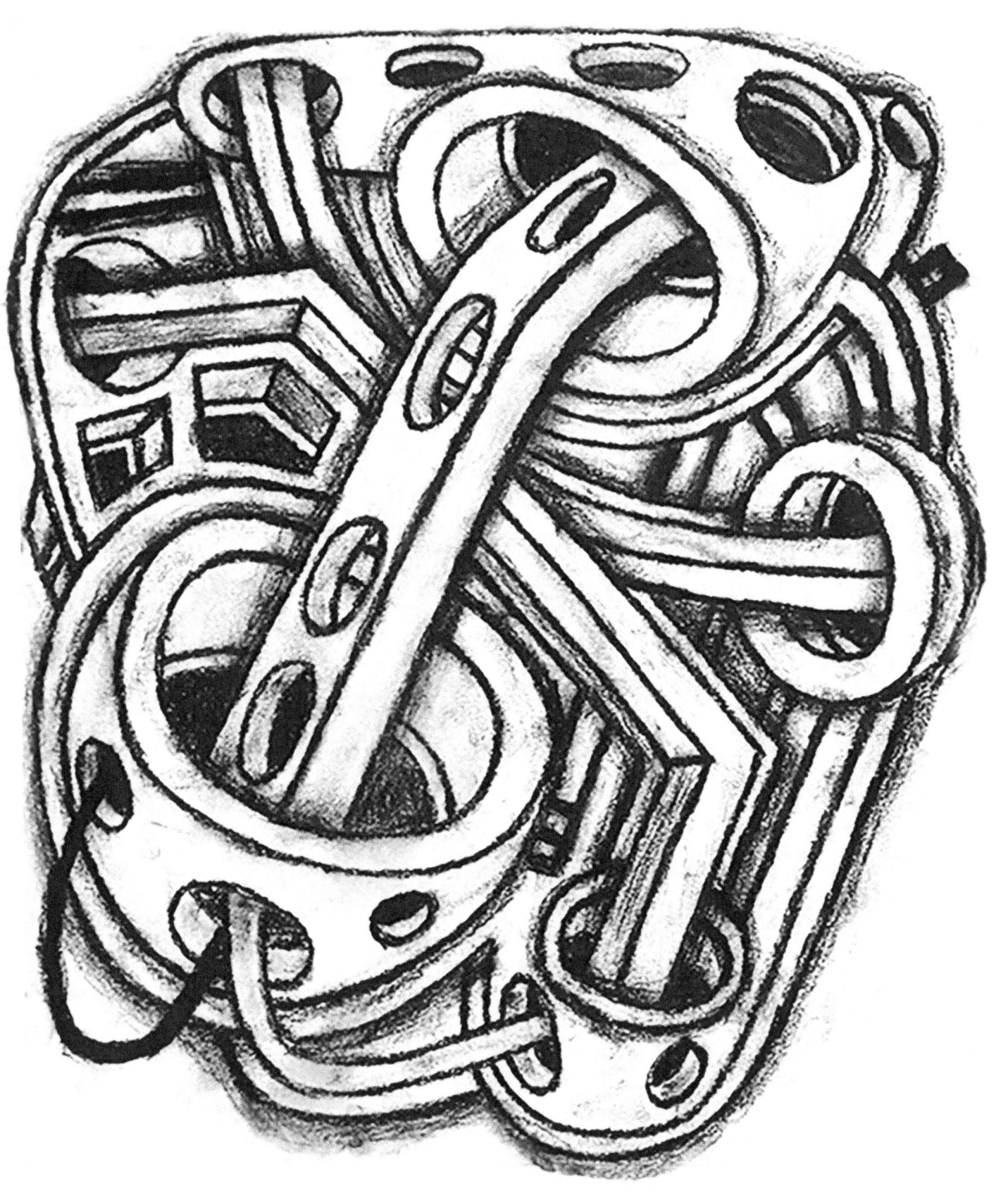

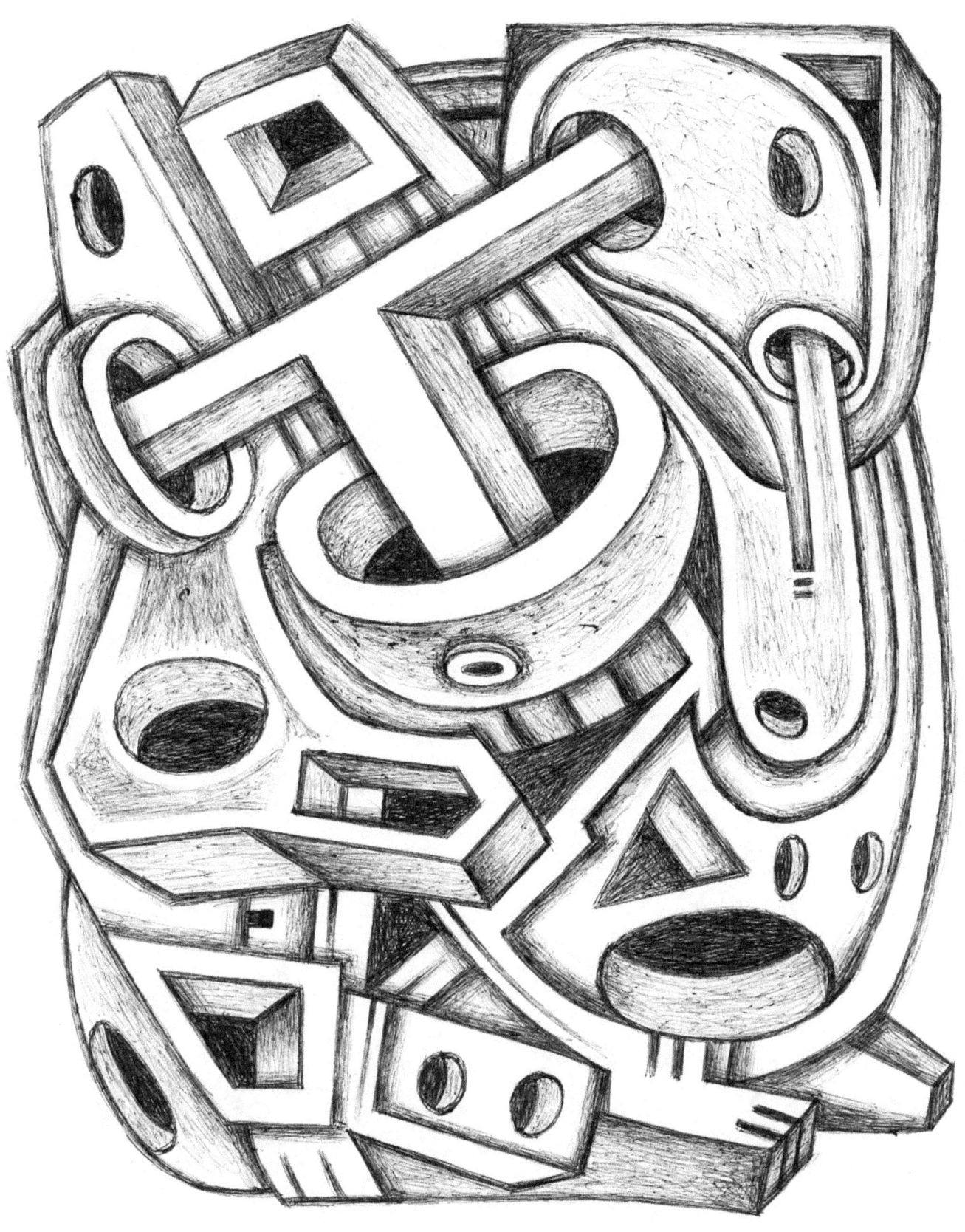

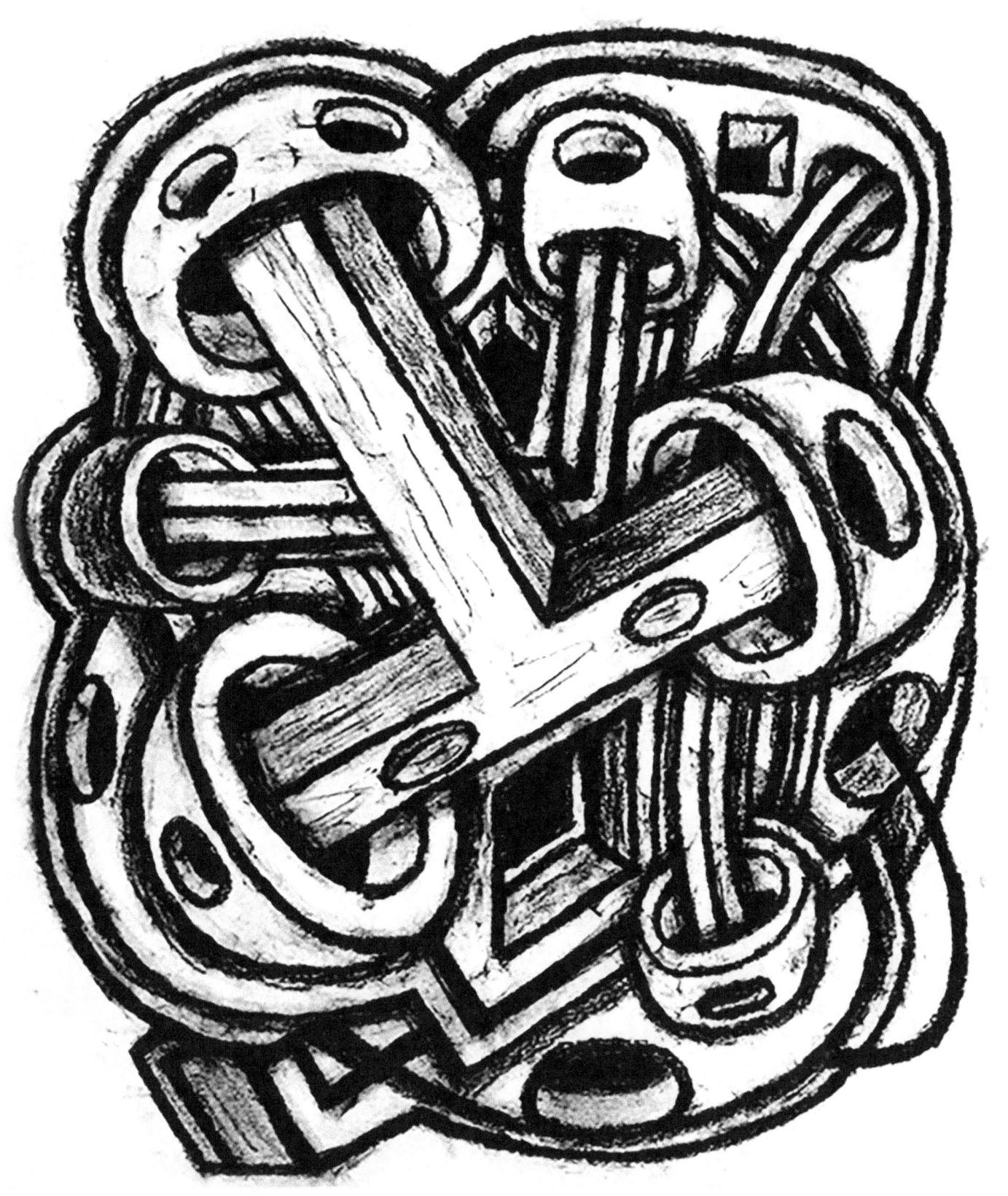

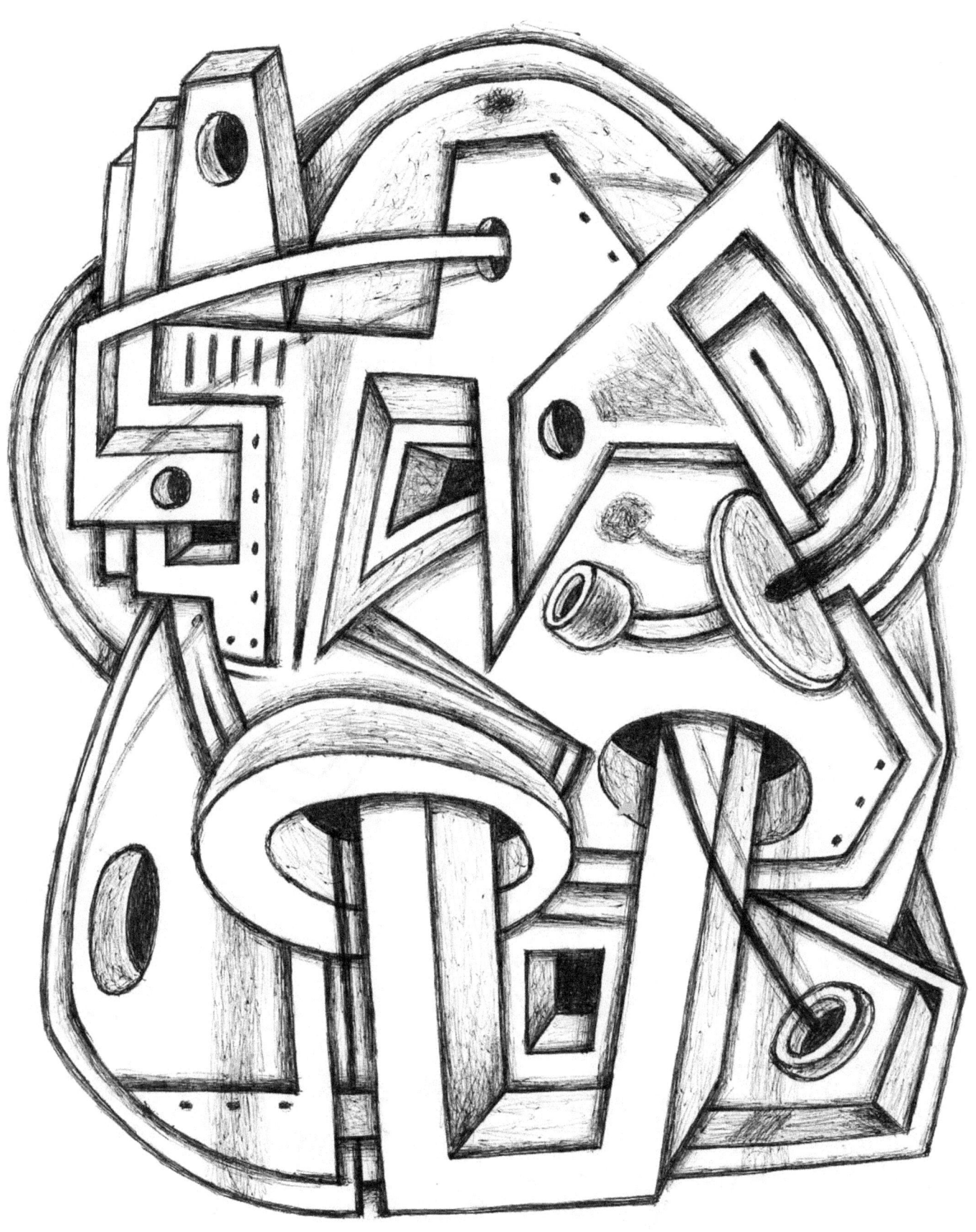

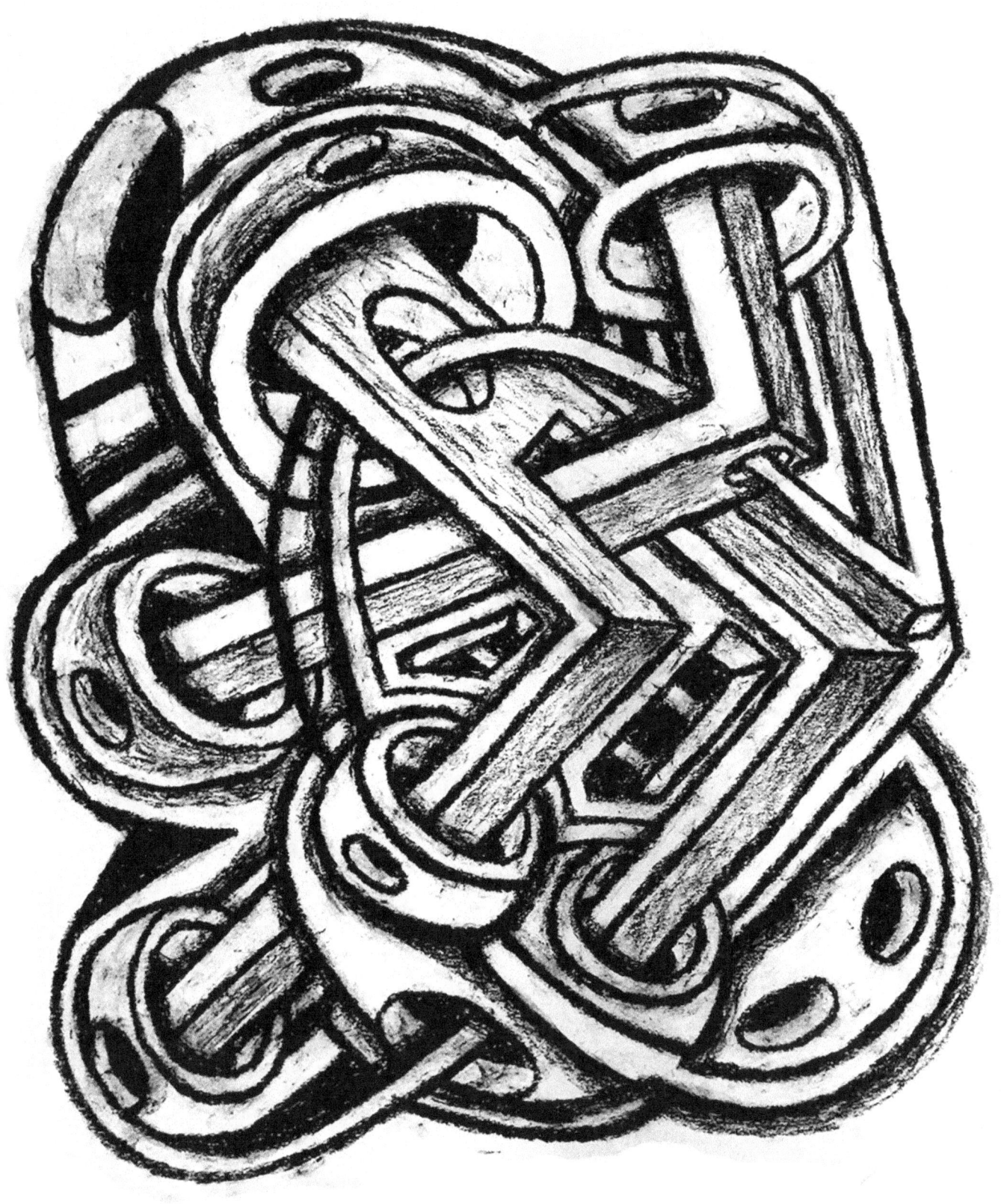

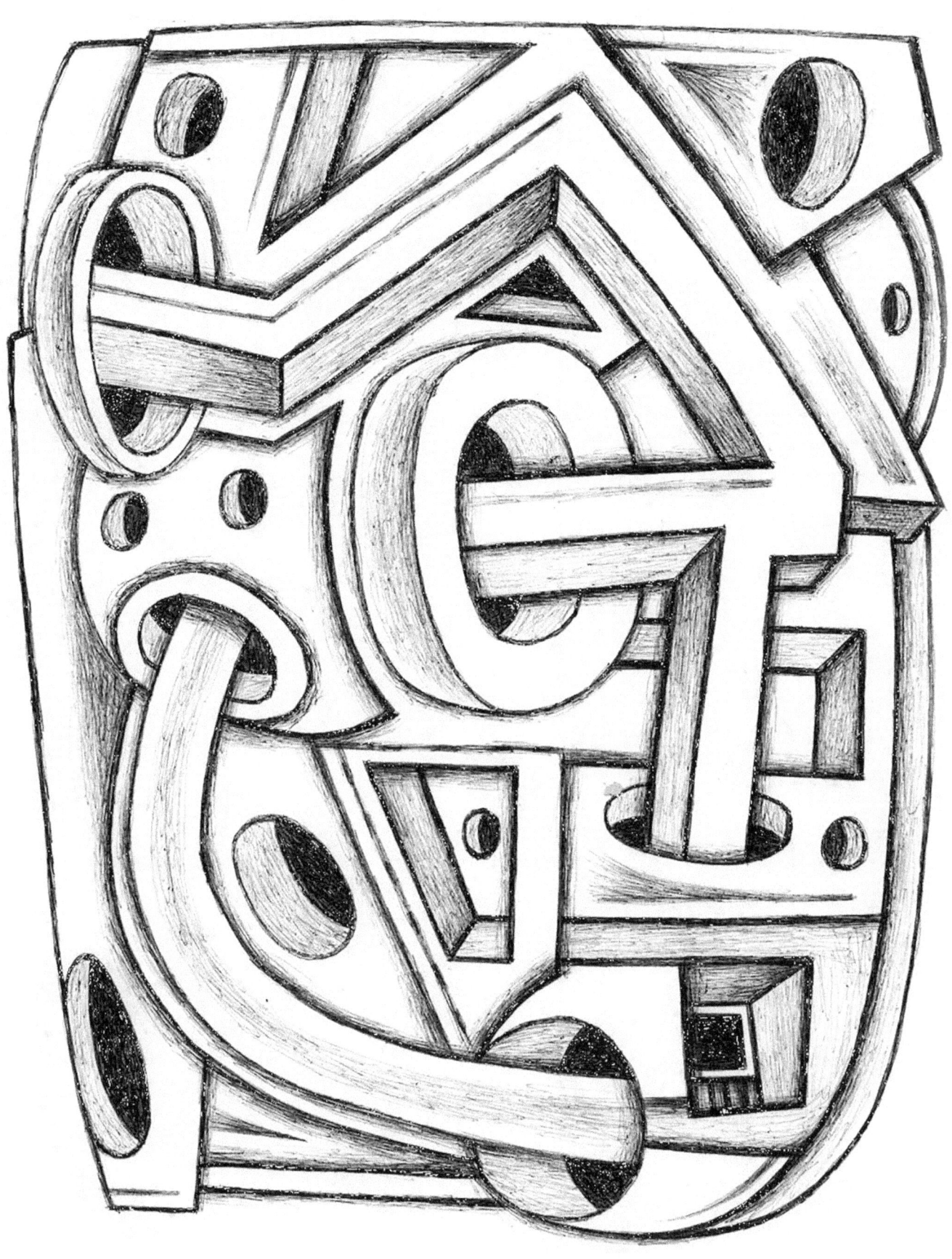

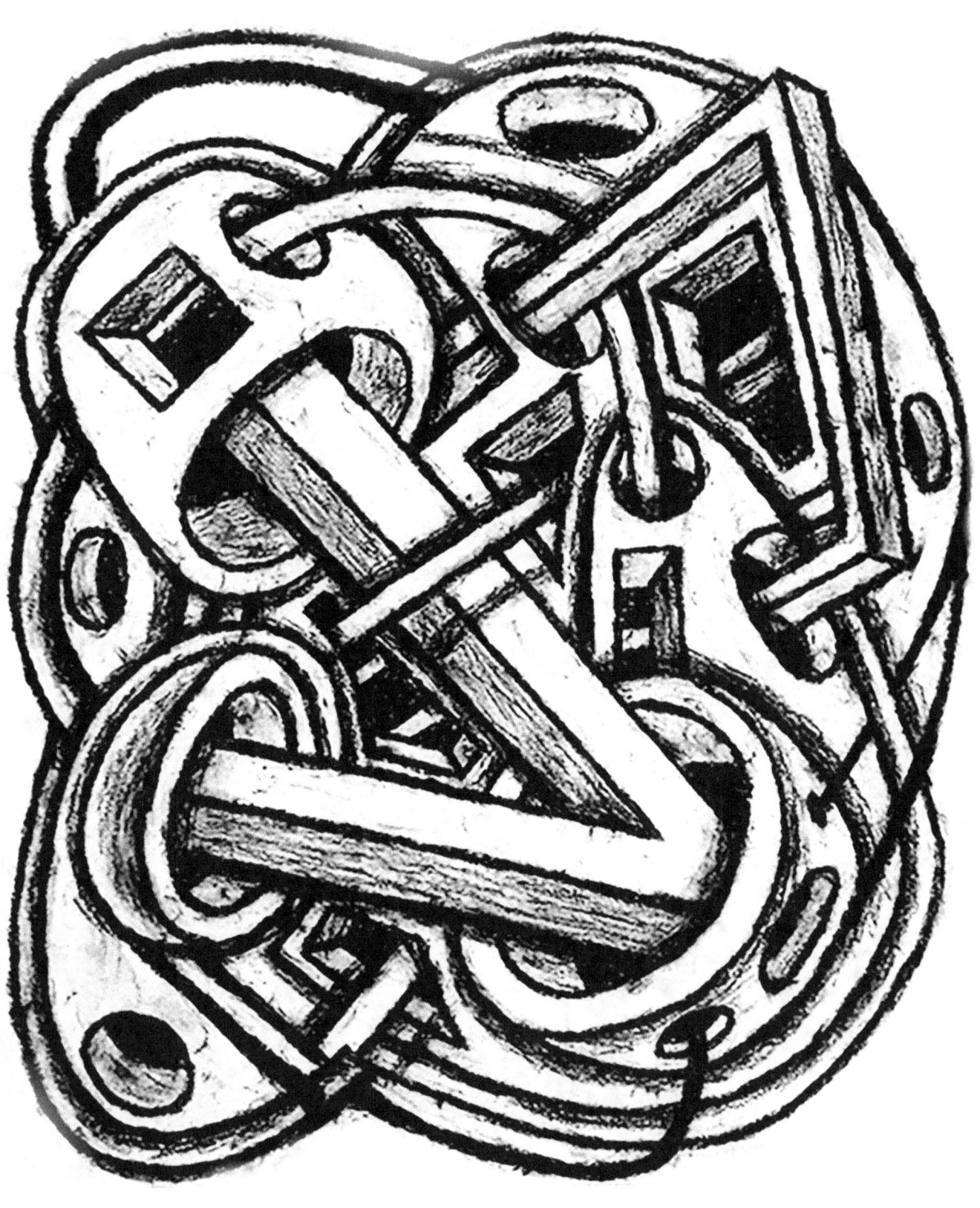

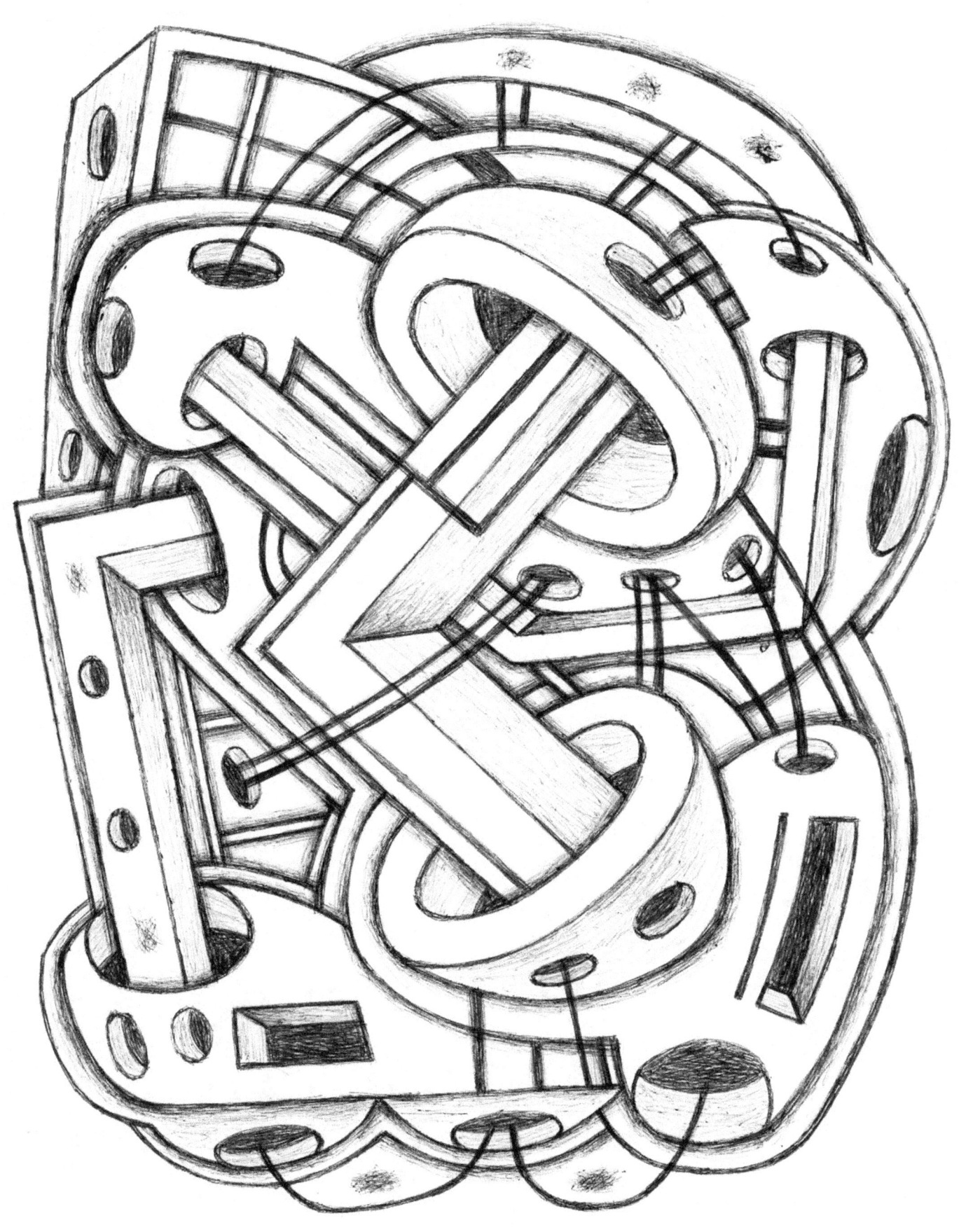

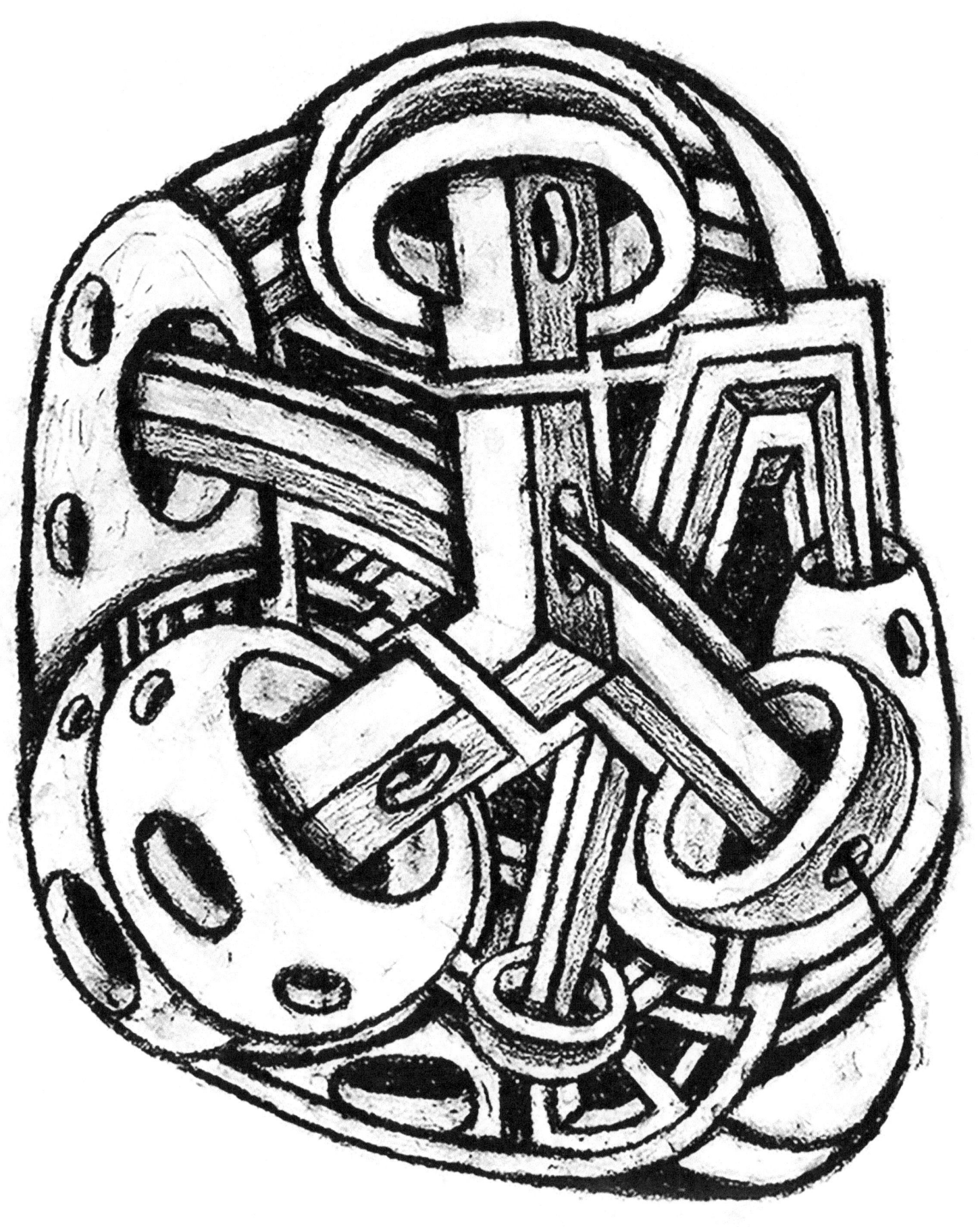

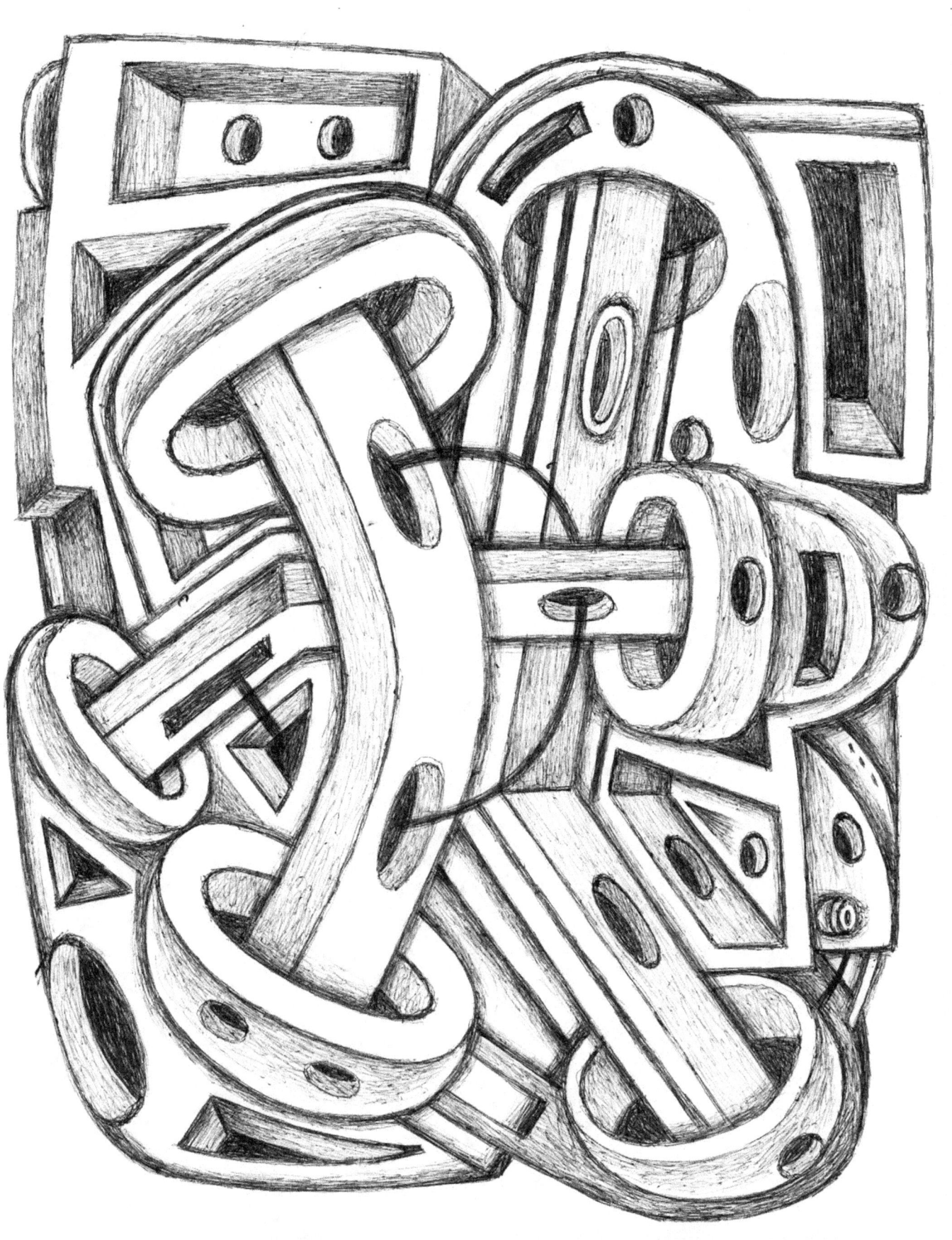

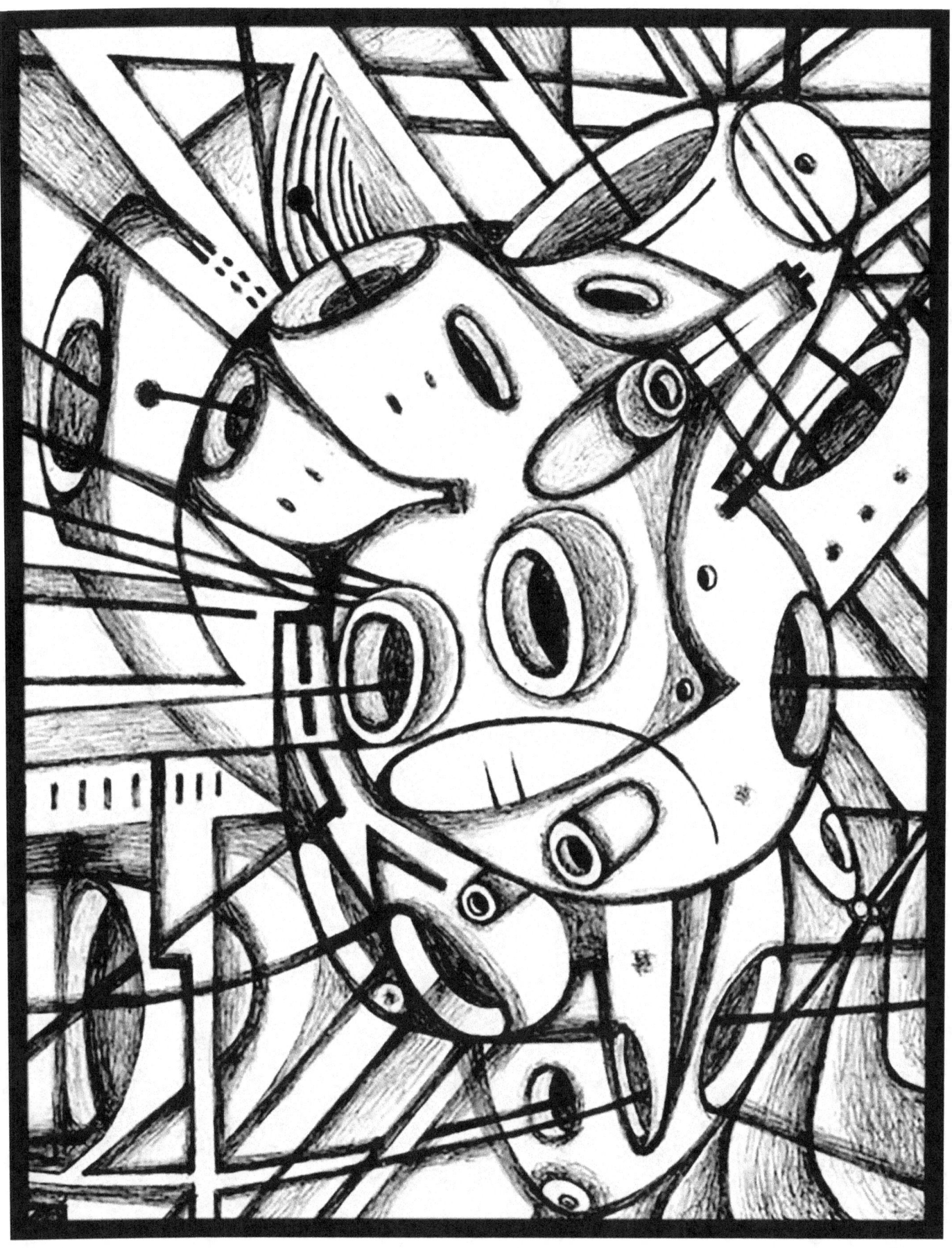

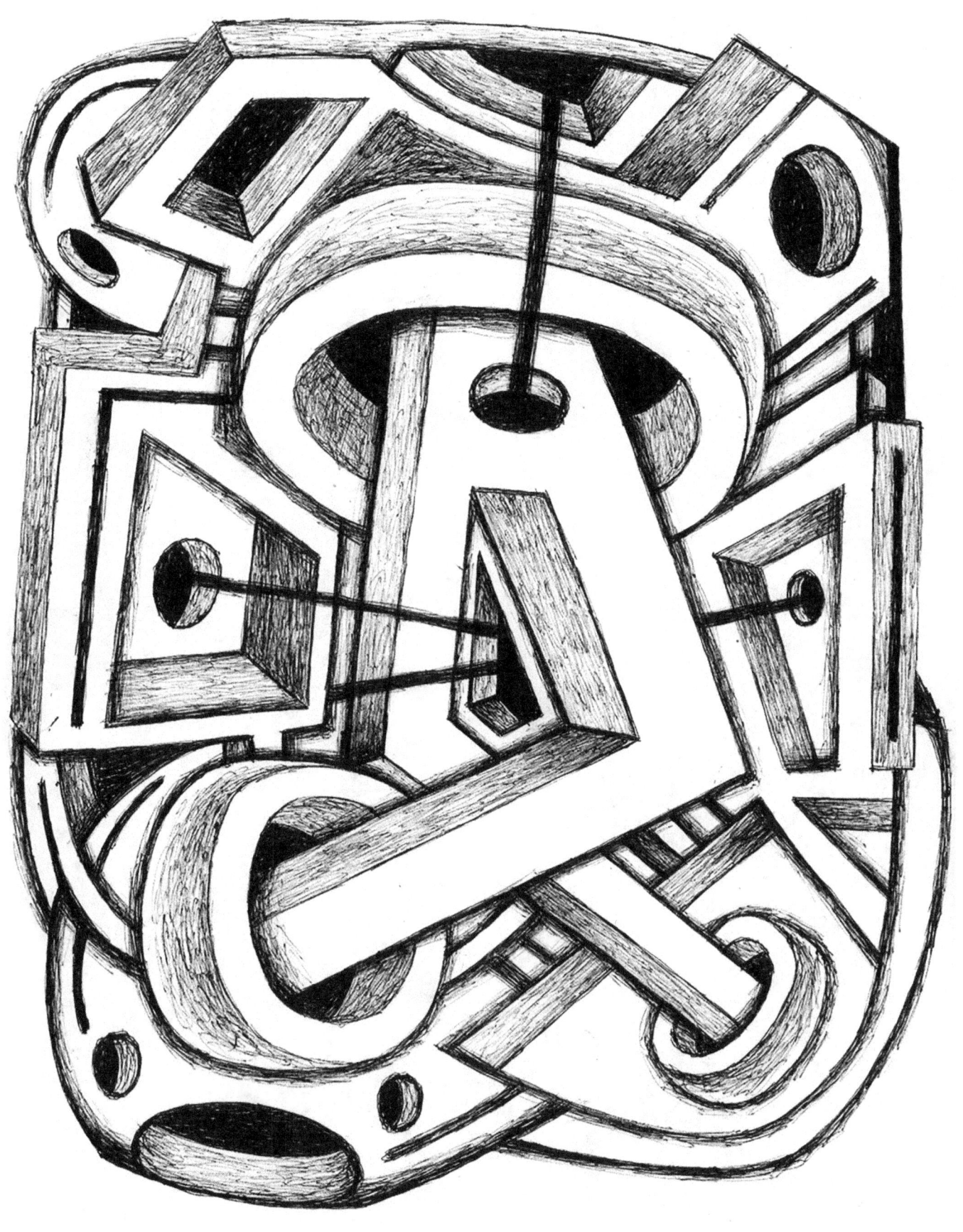

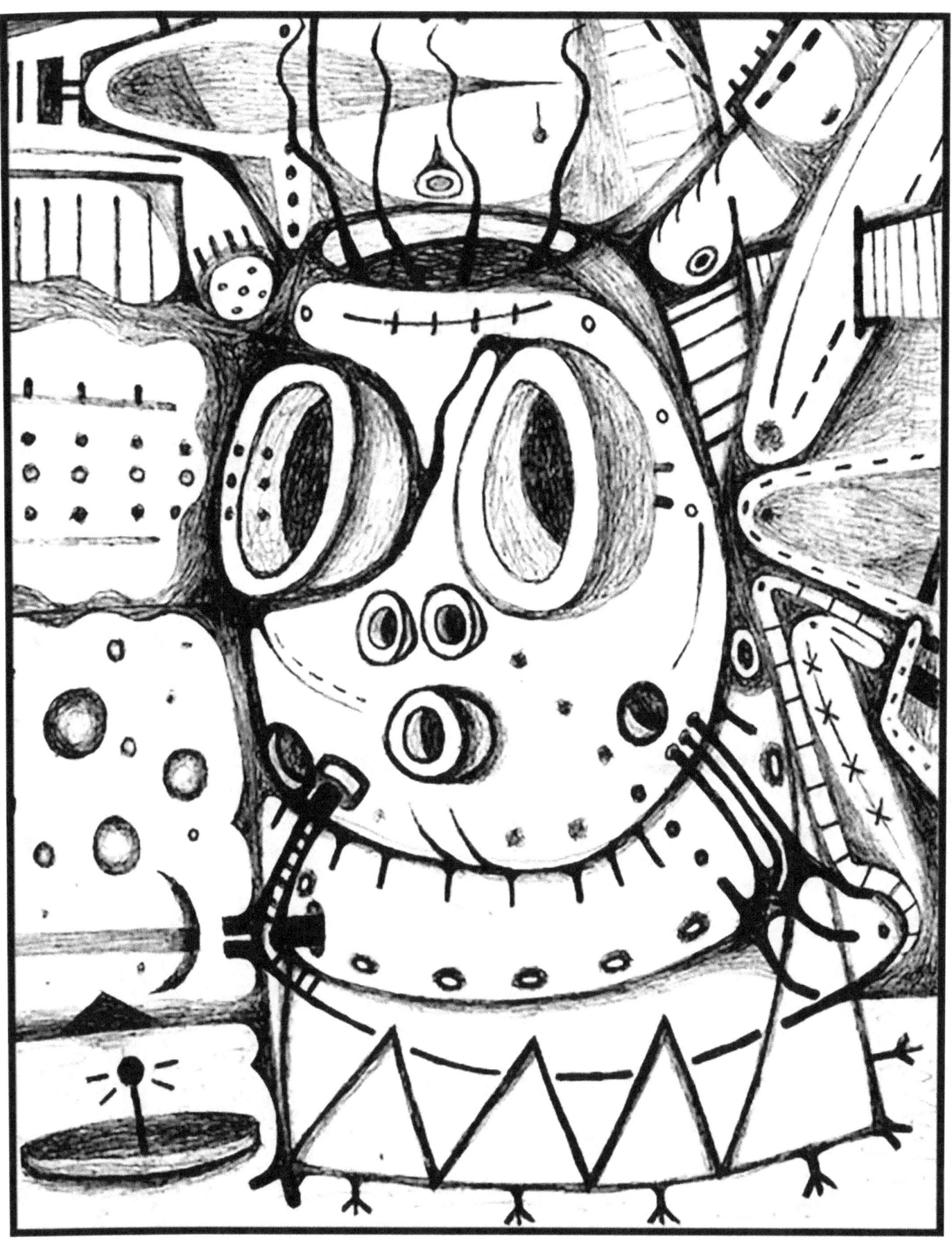

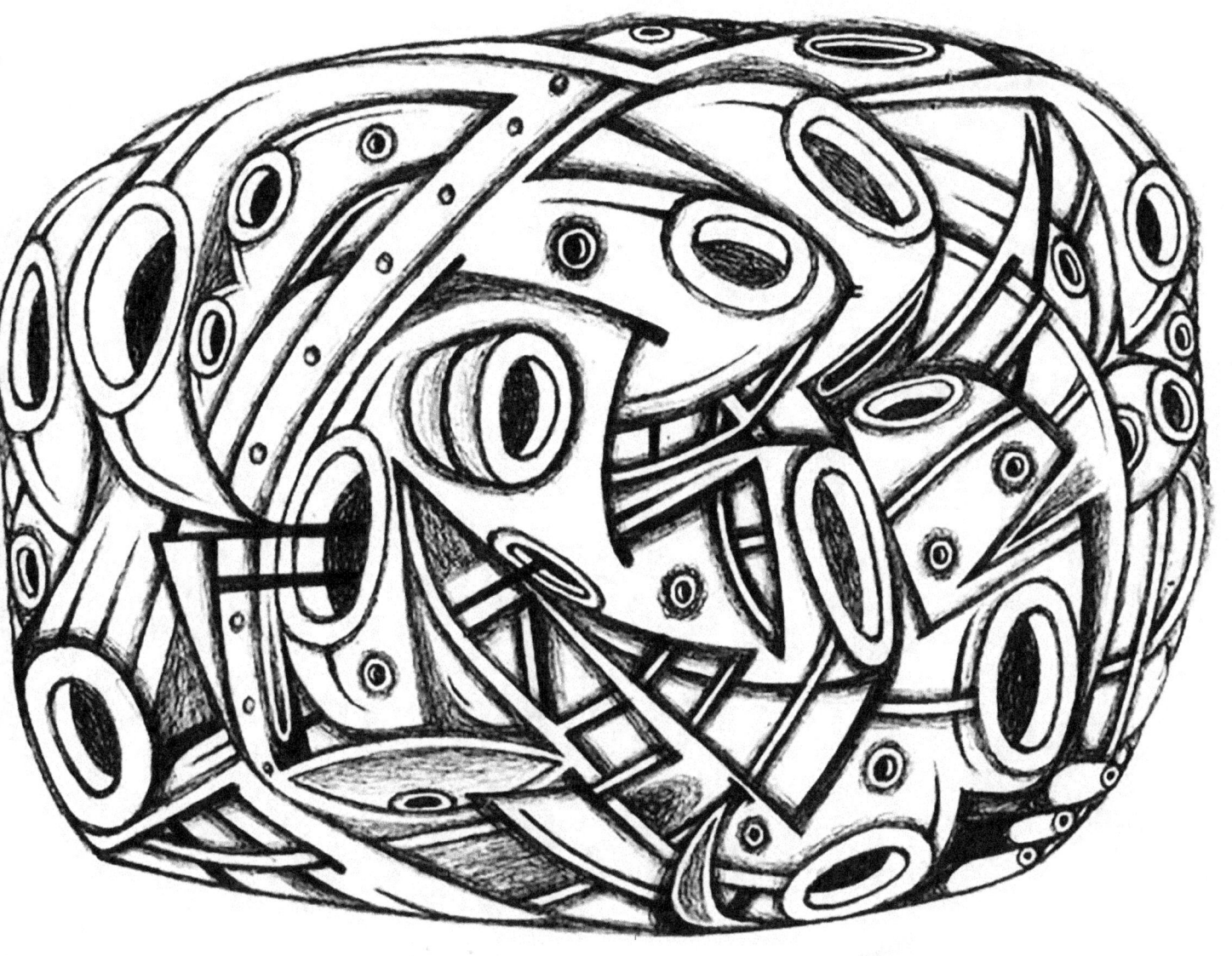

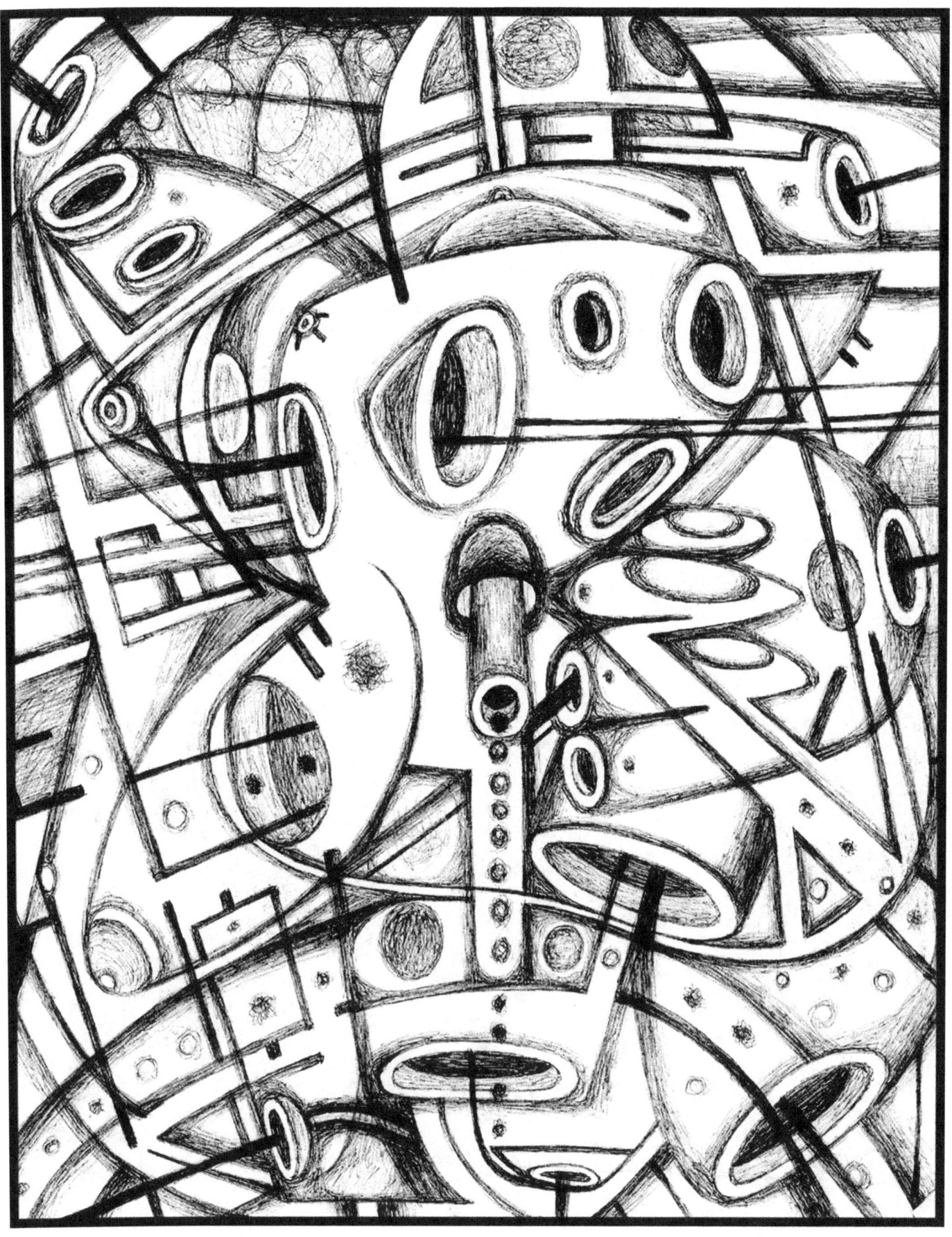

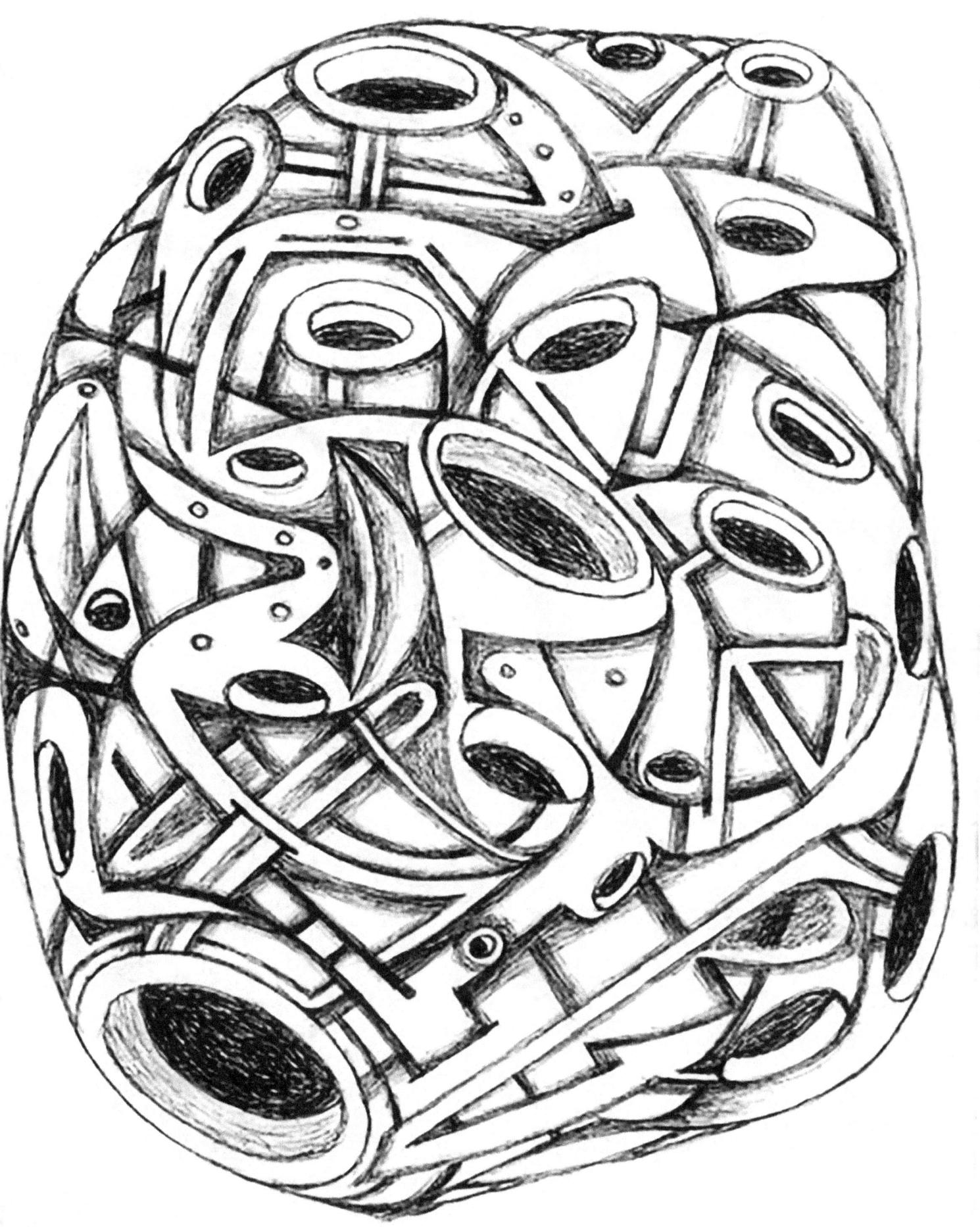

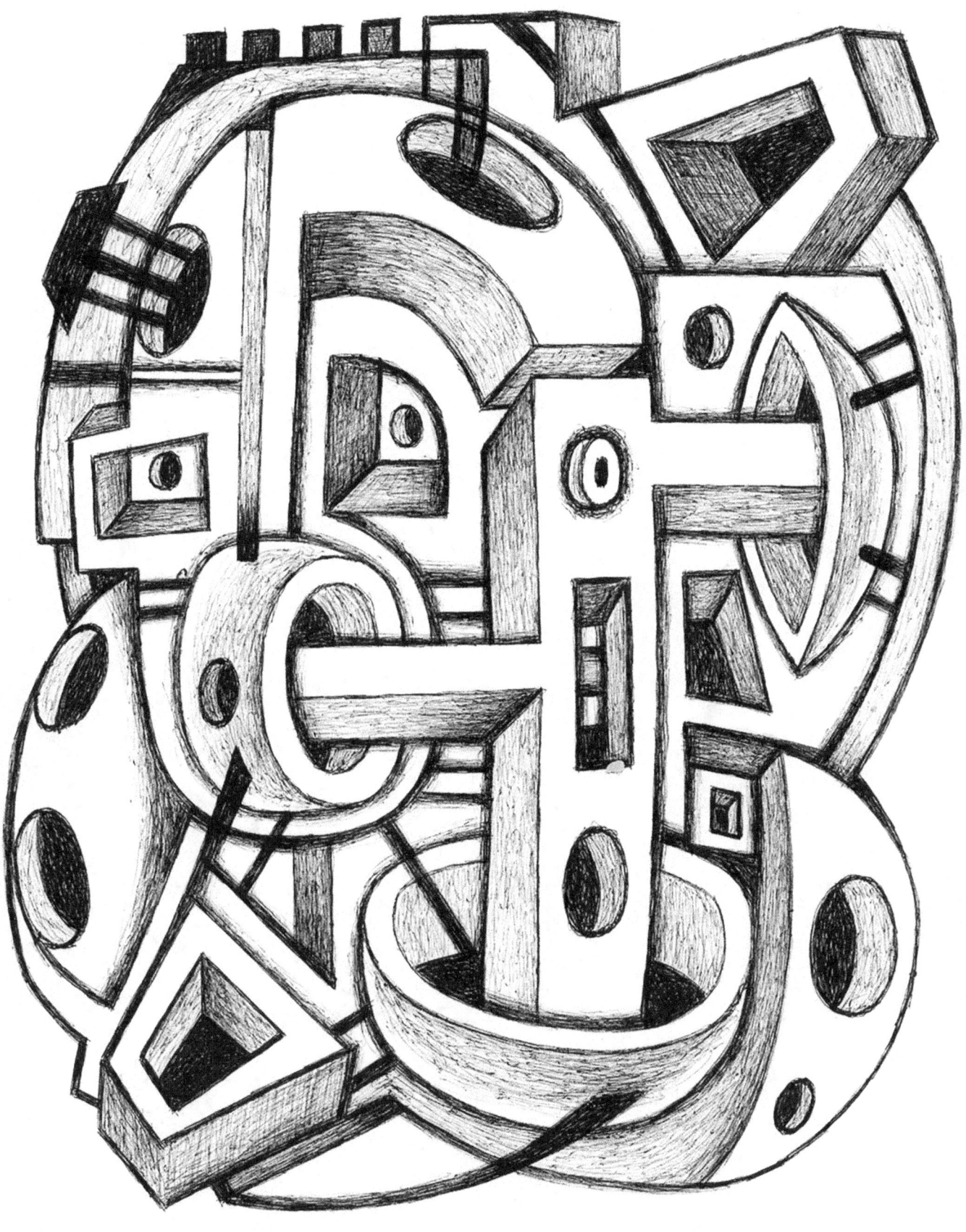

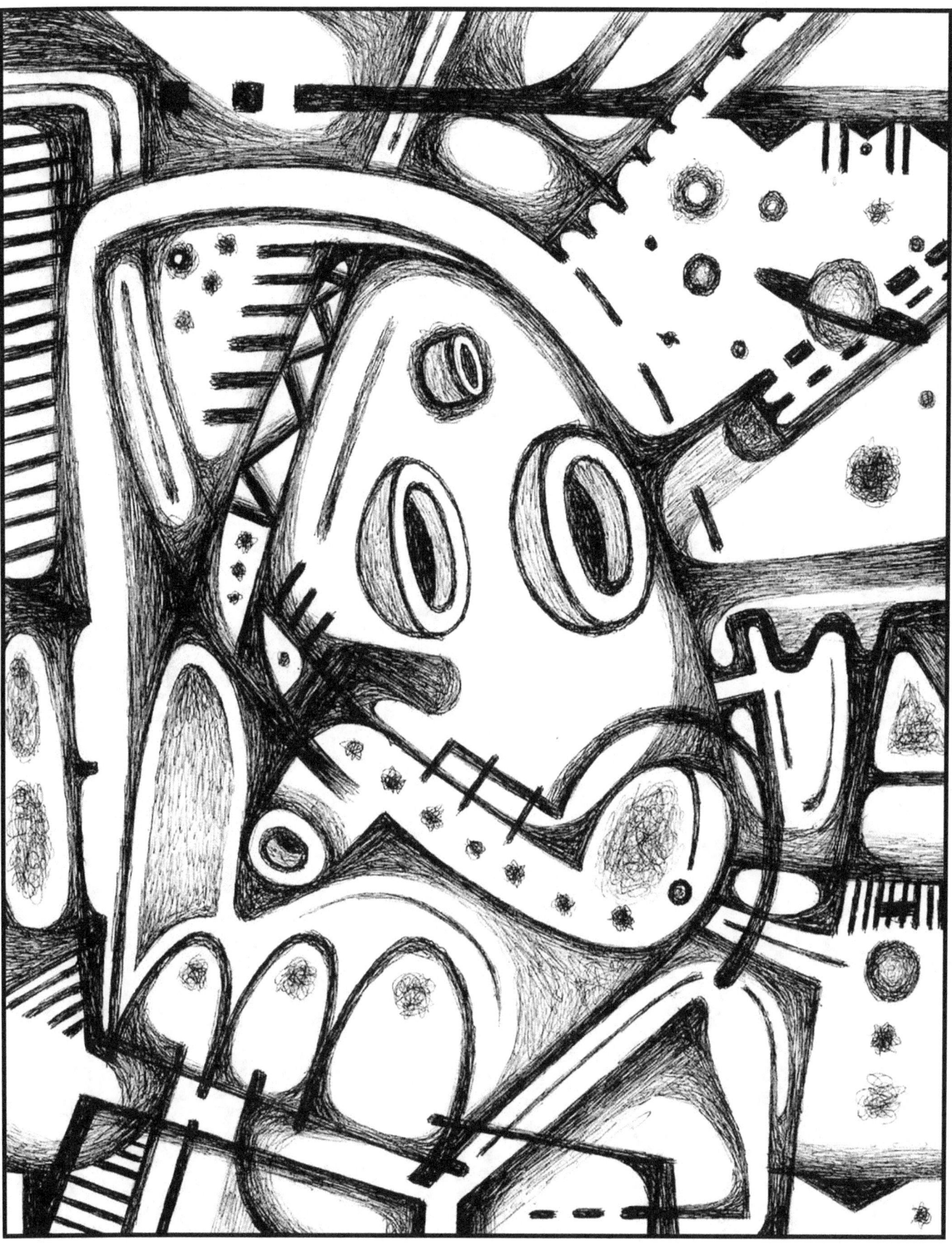

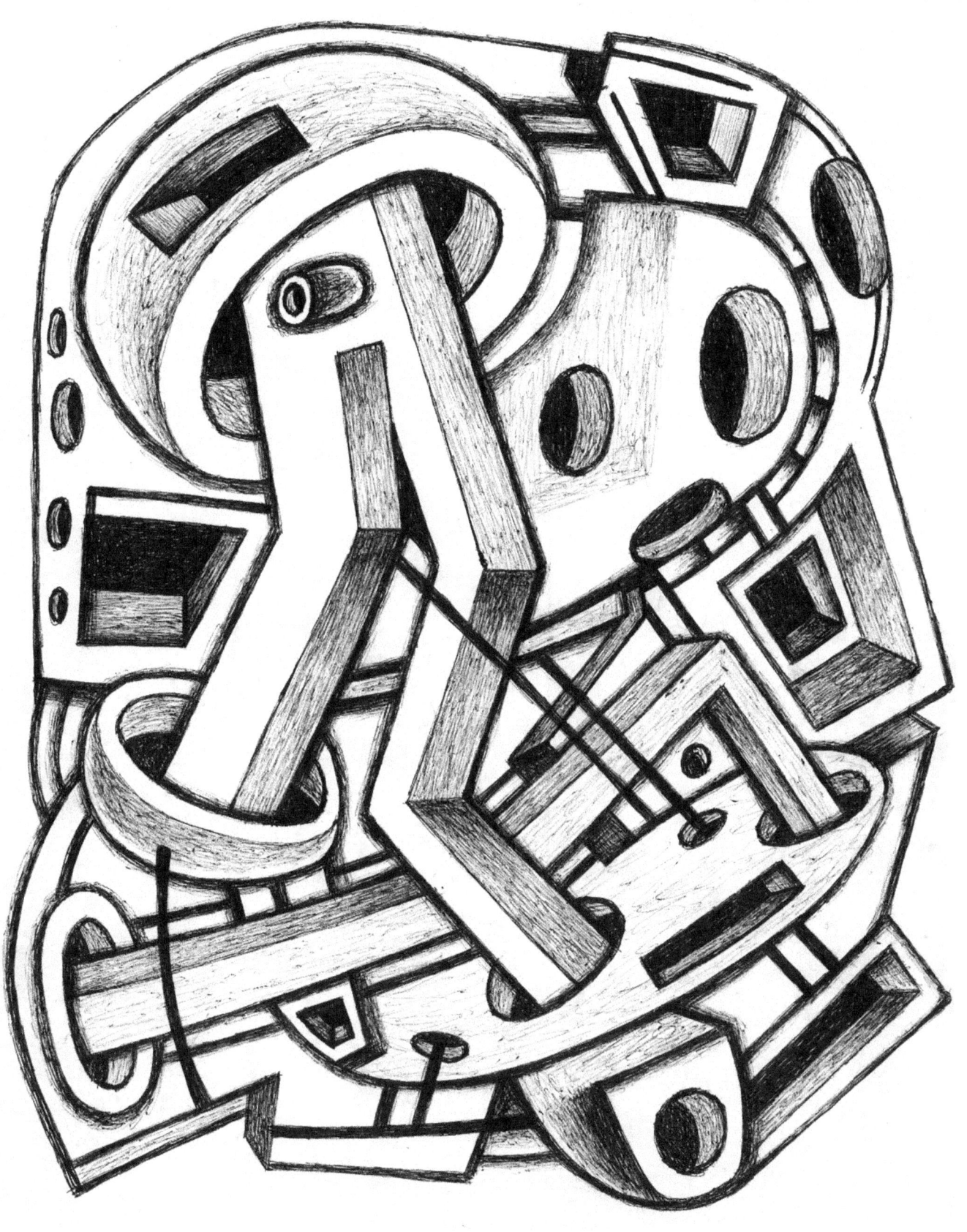

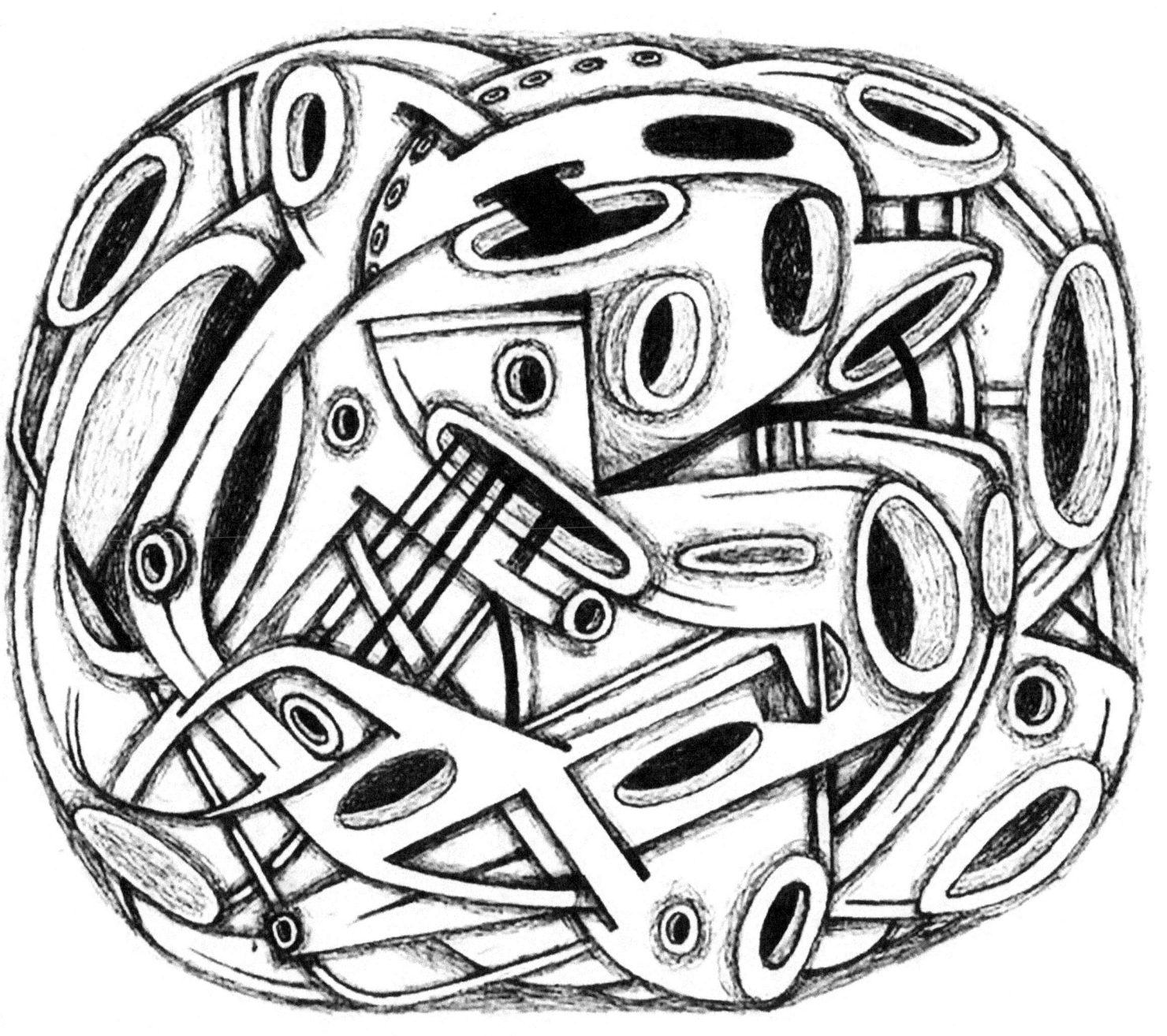